Dirty Little Secrets

&

The Little White Lie

Danielle N. Hall

DIRTY LITTLE SECRETS & THE LITTLE WHITE LIE
Copyright © 2019 by Danielle N. Hall

All rights reserved. No part of this book may be reproduced or transmitted in any form or by any means without written permission from the author.

ISBN: 978-1-7339413-0-3
Library of Congress Control Number: 2019904186

Book Cover Design: Vision to Fruition Publishing House
Photo Credit: Danielle N. Hall
Editor: Rae Williams

Printed in the USA by Vision to Fruition Publishing House (www.vision-fruition.com)

You may order copies of this book and other materials at **www.daniellenhall.com**

Dedication

This book is dedicated to anyone who has been violated and suffers in silence. May you find the light at the end of the tunnel.

Table of Contents

Foreword 1

Preface 3

Introduction 5

Chapter One – The Curious Kid 9

Chapter Two – The Touch 13

Chapter Three – The Question 19

Chapter Four – In Search Of… 23

Chapter Five – The Invitation 27

Chapter Six – Behind Closed Doors 31

Chapter Seven – The Curse 35

Chapter Eight – The Blessing 39

Appendix A – Scriptures for Healing 43

Appendix B – Songs of Healing 45

Appendix C – Poems of Healing 46

Breaking the Silence 73

About the Author 92

About the Publisher 93

Foreword

In this maze we call life, along each of our personal journeys, most, if not all of us, carry at least one secret. It's that event, action, or story that we may not want anyone to know. Sometimes, it is not our preference to share because it's OUR secret. We have deemed it our personal business, that if shared with someone, there is the belief that the unveiling of that secret may change either how someone views us or feels about us. It's hard to discern who to trust with our secrets. Will they tell someone? Secrets can sometimes carry shame, fear, and torment. But in the pages you're about to read, Danielle freely shares what some may view as a *"dirty little secret."* She seamlessly unveils the secrets in a way that doesn't bring shame but reveals truth. It confronts a dark past in order to bring to light a bright future.

Dirty Little Secrets reveals a treasured truth which brings liberation – a true freedom that will set others free who read it. May you absorb what's shared and feel safe to reveal your truth. This book confidently assures that you are not alone in this life's journey.

There's no shame. There's no bondage. There is only freedom.

Min. Michelle D. Bennett

Preface

As of late I find myself repeatedly using "f" words. One in particular has become quite frequent in my day to day conversations. In this book, you will find the use of, or reference to many "f" words: family, fear, and faith are a few. Over the last year, I've been motivated to drop that major "f" bomb with many people. I had previously held my tongue, but like Byron Cage: I can't hold it! I mean the more I thought about things people had done and said over the years, that "f" bomb kept on rising up, but I refused to drop it. I finally let down my guard and let that bomb drop. You have no idea how many people and offenses were worthy of it. I mean, I know some people have dropped it on me and we do reap what we sow. Finally, I had to drop my pride and let those who despitefully used me and who spoke ill of me have it! I released an "I FORGIVE YOU" and began to discover my freedom. I had to take a page from my debut book Dew Drops: Refreshing for the Soul: "When you forgive you take the weight off of your shoulders, the strain off of your heart, and the shackles off of your feet".

Though this book will recount the accounts of a series of unfortunate experiences, its ending conveys a different message. It is a true story of ups and downs, but it ends on a high note. One of the challenges of life is trying to locate the light in a dark place. I have discovered that light and I hope that this memoir will be a source of hope and light for those who read it and will help to liberate those who have been bound by the weight of the secrets they have been holding on to for years or by the weight of unforgiveness.

Introduction

I can't believe what "he" did to me
It's truly a crying shame
Who is this "he" you might be asking
Well, there are too many to name

"He" touched me when I was little
In places that were meant for my spouse
I was nervous AND I was afraid
Yet I remained as quiet as a mouse

"He" asked me "Are you ready?"
Inside, I had screamed no
I wanted to run, but was paralyzed by fear
And I could not manage to go

"He" didn't have a knife
Nor did he hold a gun to my head
He did stand there ready to conquer
But used manipulation instead

"He" whispered in my minor ears
And said, "If it's all night, it's all right!"
The next day we entered a secluded place that was void of both safety and light

"He" kissed me and then "he" asked
"Do you want me to put it in?"
I was very confused, yet I refused
However, the next day "he" tried again

Now, this time I didn't refuse
And decided "Ok. We'll try."
Once again, I'd been manipulated
But now by another guy

When it was over, I thought to myself
"Ok. I made it through."
Later I thought: "What in the world have I done? What did I get myself into?"
I actually thought "he" loved me
How silly was I and what was I thinking?
I was in too deep, and in a deep sleep...
Was intoxicated, yet I wasn't drinking

Exposed to so much before it was time, but convinced I had things under control
To myself I had lied. I was broken inside, but on the outside, I appeared to be whole.

My smile is now real and there's a difference in how I feel.
What I've shared is a piece of my "THEN"
My history had me bound and holding my head down, but NOW I've got my smile again

Dirty Little Secrets & The Little White Lie

That monster called "he", may have stolen something from me...something that wasn't for the taking
But God has restored the years and dried those inner tears
Inside my heart is no longer breaking

I'm daily renewed with a new point of view
I'm still here to tell my story
Those bad things that happened will work for my good and, somehow, God will get the glory

I could be bitter, I could be depressed
As a matter of fact, that was the old me
I've gotten my joy back and a new hold on life
I thank God I'm totally free!!!

The secret is out...no more shame or doubt. From now on I vow to be bold.
I will hold my head high...in spite of the fact...
This is one of the hardest true stories I've ever told.

(Dirty Little Secrets & the Little White Lie© originally written and published by Danielle N. Hall on 4/26/2016 - Danielle's Place Blog)

Danielle N. Hall

Chapter One
The Curious Kid

Growing up as an only child in my house, I learned to find things to keep me content and occupied. Most of the time I made decisions to do something productive, while other times I engaged in some very interesting activities: like mixing powder and water in toy cups and setting the child table up so that my doll babies and I could have a tea party. I want to be careful not to give the impression that my parents did not spend time with me. As a matter of fact, we often played games together. Yahtzee was one of my favorites. We would also watch game shows like Jeopardy and Wheel of Fortune. When time and opportunity permit, I still enjoy Jeopardy and will call my mom so that we may compete via phone. Yahtzee taught me a lot about strategy and Jeopardy helps me obtain information that I did not know and apply the knowledge that I possess in multiple areas. When we see that there is a category referencing the human body or health my mom usually says "Oh, Lord" because she knows that I'm likely to get those answers right…or know those questions I should say. I'll explain why in just a moment, but I really wanted to point out that though I did (and still do) enjoy time alone, I did (and do) have enjoyable moments with my family.

I was a curious child and am an inquisitive adult. As a little girl, I remember trying on my mothers' bra and stuffing it with bathroom tissue. I was in the bathroom and she eventually knocked on the door and I hurried and threw the bra in the bathtub. I'm not sure why that's what I chose to do, but I had to think on my toes and my options were few. Of course, my mom knew the deal, but fortunately I did not receive any harsh punishment for my curiosity. Much of my curiosity led me to books. I recall specifically being fond of the Better Homes & Garden Family Medical Guide which happened to be published in 1973: 5 years before my birth. I was especially drawn to two sections in particular: the reproductive system & pregnancy and childbirth. There is something about the human body and the miracle of life that have always been intriguing to me. I seemed to concentrate on the full menstrual cycle and the stages of pregnancy. Oddly enough, I wasn't compelled to become an obstetrician, but I desired to become a pediatrician specializing in neonatology: a subspecialty of pediatrics that consists of the medical care of newborn infants, especially the ill or premature newborn. This was my desire until my junior high school year of high school, when my career goal became Physical Therapy. That career goal eventually shifted as well, and I decided to work in the field of child development.

One of my favorite childhood toys was The Little Professor. It was a product released by Texas Instruments in 1976. When you turned it on, you would have to choose a difficulty level and then an equation would appear. I really enjoyed this device and I enjoyed learning and discovering new things. Just as eager as I was (and am) to learn, I'm equally eager to share with others what I learn. I had a keepsake book as a child that was labeled "School Days" on the outside. It was a keepsake to follow you from Kindergarten through high school graduation. I remember the section asking what we wanted to be when we grew up. There were multiple choices and I'd always check the boxes beside doctor and teacher. I like to consider myself now as more of an enlightener: as one who encourages others to be inquisitive and to discover a world of information outside of their present scope of knowledge. I believe that some of the smartest people are not those who have all the answers, but who both know and understand that they don't and go on a quest to learn and live and then live and learn. Some of my lessons weren't learned in the school house, but through experiences in the school of life. Some of these experiences I will journey through in the remainder of the pages in this memoir.

Danielle N. Hall

Chapter Two
The Touch

One of the things I used to love about Saturday mornings was getting up early and not having to go to school. Though I thoroughly enjoyed school, I also enjoyed the break known as the weekend. Saturday morning cartoons were the best! Don't sleep on The 3 Stooges, either. When I was MUCH younger, I thought those guys were hilarious. Fortunately, I wasn't a couch potato. As a matter of fact, for recreation many of the children from the neighborhood would gather outside and engage in friendly fun. We'd play well known childhood games like Tag, Freeze Tag, Hide and Seek, and we'd jump rope. Double-dutch was one of my favorites and was not for the fearful: especially when they got to "S-K-I-N, SKIN!!!" You knew that rope was getting ready to be turned in turbo mode and you had better keep those feet moving to keep up with the speed of the rope or you'd wind up with a bunch of whelps on your legs. The other tricky thing about double-dutch was when you had a person turning the rope who was double handled. If you were good enough, this wasn't a big issue, but certainly could present a challenge for the beginner.

I loved the games and jumping rope, but I was not courageous enough to actually learn how to skate. After having failed in my first attempt that resulted in me both falling and getting a right-angle shaped tear in my new jumper, I decided that may not be the best choice for me. Time would go by before I would get up the nerve to try again, and that didn't go over so well either. The setting the first time was outside of my apartment on the concrete and the second failed attempt was at the skating rink to celebrate the birthday of one of my little cousins. By the time I had reached halfway around the rink, I had fallen three times and hurt my lower back. I did not feel compelled to subject myself to further discomfort, so I actually quit. Moving forward, each time the school had a skating trip I declined and would stay at the school. Oh, the memories!

Speaking of memories, one of many memories that I'll share in this book comes to mind. So, about those "f" words mentioned previously...It was always fun being creative and spending time outdoors with neighborhood friends, but it was just as enjoyable to spend time with family. I mean there's nothing like it! When I was in the latter part of my elementary school years, I would spend time at the home of a nearby relative. I loved children and there were four who lived there at the time. At a very young age, I grew fond of nurturing others and helping others to learn. Actually, I used to be the math tutor for one of my peers that lived in the neighborhood. As I mentioned before, since childhood, I aspired to be a doctor or a teacher. That still is sorta the case: I have a deep passion for helping others to be well and for helping others to be enlightened. I even attended Howard University's College of Allied Health Sciences for three years in pursuit of a Master of Science in Physical Therapy (MSPT) Degree. Due to financial challenges during that time, I turned to my other love: teaching. I worked at two different child care centers and while at the second center, I earned the Preschool Child Development Associate (CDA) Credential. I had not long after conceived my second child. The pregnancy was difficult, and I chose to return to an environment that would be less demanding and would induce the least amount of stress. I pursued employment as a medical receptionist because it was in an environment that I was both familiar with and comfortable with.

I digress.

Let's get back to me visiting with my family member with the children. The children were all boys and two were infants. The older boys were pretty active, and I found myself disciplining one of the two older boys quite a bit. I'd walk the eldest to school. We attended the same school: he was in kindergarten and I was in the 5th grade. I'd pick him up on school mornings and bring him home in the afternoon. He was fairly quiet and wasn't any trouble. We'd arrive at his house and I'd get to feed, play with, and rock the babies. I can't fully express in words how much of a delight this privilege was for me. It was both fun and fulfilling to get to witness and be a part of my family growing up. Weekends were the best because I could spend more time with the boys and their mom! Sometimes, their mom would still be asleep when I would go over on weekend mornings.

I recall one Saturday morning going over to the house early before the boys' mom was up. She and her companion were still in bed. They had a friend over and the friend answered the door. I had one of my little cousins with me who was three years old at the time. I sat at the dining table while my little cousin played under the table. The boys were not up yet either, so I waited for everyone to get up and come out of their rooms. I'd soon find myself being accompanied at the table by this family friend. He sat in a chair next to me. He didn't say a word. His next move was to place his hands between my legs. Fortunately, I had on pants. I was frozen and speechless, but I eventually mustered up enough courage to speak just above a whisper: "Can you please not touch me?" I was frightened…meanwhile, my three-year-old cousin had stated that she had to use the bathroom and I had the paralyzing thought that this man would follow us to the bathroom. So, I let her wet herself, and used that as my way of escape back home. I felt bad because she got chastised a little bit for wetting herself, but it wasn't her fault. However, I was too afraid to tell what had happened. I was apprehensive to return to my family member's house, but I had to because I had school walking responsibilities. I was afraid, but I was wiser in the time of day I'd go to visit. Nothing could keep me away from spending time with the boys: not even a child molester. Fortunately, He never touched me again.

Danielle N. Hall

Chapter Three
The Question

I can't say it enough: I LOVE MY FAMILY! I love the babies and I love helping to nurture them. I used to really love the newborn to five age range. It is said that this is the time span when children are most like sponges. I learned that in my training in early childhood development. I seemed to always be able to best connect with children in that age range. My family is pretty large so, I had the opportunity to connect with the wee ones. Some family I had the opportunity to spend more time with than others. I had practically moved in with one close family member. There were a few little people there that I could bond with. Now those children are much older with children of their own. As much as I loved the company and shared many laughs and had many good times, there was one situation that took place on some occasions that all started with a question: "Are you ready?" Now at the time I was about 11 years old, yet somehow, I seemed to have a good idea of what that question meant. After all, I had studied that Family Medical Guide and I had cable television at an early age. Since "the touch", something had been awakened in me that would have otherwise remained dormant. I remember the night before my 6th grade graduation I had been up all night at home watching HBO and Showtime. After hours, there definitely weren't any kid friendly shows on, so rest assured that wasn't what I was watching. There were two movies in particular that I watched: Joy of Flying and Body Heat. Both were rated "R" and contained scenes with nudity. This appetite for what we will call "junk food" was encouraged by the touch that was unauthorized by who we will call "He #1".

So, let's get back to the question posed by "He #2". I heard the question, and that paralysis of fear that I experienced with the touch from He #1 returned. Yet, I felt the safest response was yes because I did not know what was going to happen if I said no. He said he'd be right back. Apparently, he stepped out to go to the store to get a box of condoms. I did not move from the space where I was sitting on the couch. Again, I was paralyzed by fear. When he returned, he came over to the couch, motioned for me to get up, and guided me to the back room. I do not recall what I was wearing, but I know he kept his shirt on and slowly removed his bottoms. I sat on the bed, he removed my bottom clothing, and proceeded to engage in statutory rape. There were no words or sounds, or perhaps I mentally checked out of the experience to try to cope with what was occurring. Eventually it was over, and he went in the bathroom to clean himself. Afterwards, I went to do the same. I noticed that I started itching profusely where I had been penetrated. I never said anything, I just kept washing. This same kind of thing would happen on other occasions with He #2 and I would sometimes sit in a tub of cold water for relief and I'd use diaper ointment that was available because of the baby in the house. It would sometimes take several days to recover. I discovered through those experiences that I am allergic to Trojan brand condoms.

Time progressed, those occurrences had ceased, but he did one day decide to pursue again. He actually came to disturb me out of my sleep. Soon after he had awakened me, his wife (my family member) showed up in that room and yelled: "I knew it!" She was rightfully angry, but I was troubled that she was angry with me. Now that I am older and have teenaged children of my own, I realize just how much I had been manipulated and violated. Soon after I became humiliated because when the word was spread and some family members became aware, there was no embracing of me or restoration offered to me. Also, I was devastated because who was once one of my favorite close relatives, viewed me as an enemy and our relationship became strained due to the actions of a man who could not control himself.

By the point of this last event, which never went any further than him waking me up by putting his hands in the upper part of the bottoms I was wearing, I was 16 years old. I was 16, in my senior year of high school, and preparing to graduate and move on to college. The stress of this situation caused me to lose weight, not apply for any scholarships, and to only apply to one college with the help of the college counselor at my school. By God's grace I was accepted into Howard University's College of Allied

Health Sciences. No one at my school was aware of what was going on with me. I do believe that my college prep and course experiences would've been different had I not ever been posed with "the question", but I've lived and I've learned and I've learned and I've lived.

Chapter Four
In Search Of...

Soooo, about those school days at "The Real HU"...college life was a little bit different from what I experienced in my high school days when I had the opportunity to take college courses: thanks to the High School/College Internship Program (HISCIP). I was enrolled in Psychology & US History courses at Trinity College (now Trinity Washington University) located in Washington, D.C. While I had made the grades and met the necessary qualifications to be accepted into the HISCIP program, I didn't fully embrace the opportunity. I did earn a "B" in Psychology, but I couldn't really connect in US History class. Honestly, I was pre-occupied with all of the other issues going on in my life. I wasn't sure which direction I was going. I had a career goal, yet I lacked the motivation to reach it. Anyhow, Trinity's population was predominantly Caucasian and had a pretty low-key vibe. When I arrived at Howard, it was pretty much culture shock. I don't regret the experience or having attended an HBCU, but the culture was just different from the previous experience I had on another college campus. Now oddly enough, I initially desired to attend Spelman College upon graduation from high school, but my father was pretty adamant about me staying at home, so Howard it was.

While walking anywhere on campus, and especially through "The Yard" someone would hand you a flyer for an upcoming party at a night club or other location. Let me make this disclaimer: I am not suggesting that Howard was a big party, but there was a healthy balance between work and play. I was too introverted to be interested. I didn't take time to make many friends, and I often spent hours alone in "The Punchout" as I waited for my next class. I commuted daily so I didn't have anywhere to stay on campus. Alone time was fine for me, though. There was always something going on at "HU" and to the introvert, it can be a bit overwhelming: just like the lines for registration for the upcoming semester. Sometimes, you'd be standing in a line for hours only to find out you'd been in the wrong line all along. It was a lively campus with people from diverse backgrounds who networked and excelled academically, which is why Howard is called the Mecca. Homecoming is one of the most popular annual campus events to take place at The Mecca. I steered clear of most large crowd events because I felt like it was too chaotic. However, the real issue wasn't the noisy, active life on campus. It was the inner noise: an internal environment full of chaos, trying to find my place because I had experienced so much at an early age that made me feel out of place. I was a child who had been exposed to what adults do, but then I was transitioning into becoming more independent, yet I still felt like a little child. I wanted to just curl up in a corner most times and be left alone, but I couldn't because I had an image to uphold. I was the honor roll student who had dreams of soon becoming a doctor, yet I was in need of healing myself. I felt perplexed, but I managed to function while internally searching for wholeness. I made the Dean's List the first semester: I was the perfect student, struggling with the imperfection of a fragmented heart and a broken spirit. I was in search of a remedy and didn't have the wherewithal to turn to the right source. I wasn't suicidal, yet I didn't like my life.

Danielle N. Hall

Chapter Five
The Invitation

In my elementary and junior high school years, some referred to me as "the teacher's pet". It's not that I sought to win favor of the teachers, but I typically found myself being shown favor and some personally took me under their wings. Many of my teachers I had the privilege of developing a personal relationship with and they are my friends even today. As a matter of fact, I'm blessed to say that I still have a great relationship with my kindergarten and first grade teachers! They have been present for so many life events for me and I count it a privilege to still have them in my life. Among the list of former teachers, now friends, is my 3rd grade art teacher. An artist in her own right and in addition to releasing her own music; she has had the privilege to share the stage with many musical greats and the esteemed honor to be a part of a world-renowned gospel singing group and remains humble. I certainly consider it a privilege and a pleasure to have such great people in my life to call friend. I even remained to connected to one who served as a student teacher in my 8th grade year. She has since relocated to the southern states but is very much still a part of my life. I recall the day she was leaving our school, my teachers had given me a pass so that I could spend the day with her and when the school day was over, she took me to McDonald's where I ordered a double cheeseburger, a small fry, and a small strawberry milkshake. She then gave me a ride home. I cried so much because she wasn't just leaving our school, but she was leaving to continue her education in a different state. I was 12 years old, but I remember like it was yesterday.

My memory also serves me well as it relates to another teacher who apparently grew fond of me. This teacher was very well liked by other teachers and by students: because of the knowledge that the teacher possessed and also the personality. It didn't hurt that the teacher was what one would describe as being "easy on the eyes". This teacher never really said much to me, but I vividly recall the day when we were in an assembly in the auditorium at the end of the day. The teacher happened to be sitting in the last seat on the row which was next to me on my right. For some strange reason he felt both comfortable and compelled to whisper in my ear: "If it's all night, it's all right." Now instead of my little 12-year-old self being clueless, I knew exactly what "it" he was referring to. I was a bit surprised, but I didn't show it in my face. When the assembly was over and we were released to our lockers and classrooms to get our belongings so that we may prepare for dismissal. I retrieved my belongings and I returned to the teacher with a clever response to what he whispered in my ear:" If it's all day it's ok." I think he was taken aback yet intrigued by my response. I was consequently given the assignment to go home and write down everything I knew about sex. I returned the next morning with a two paged, front and back paper in response to his request. He was even more taken aback. He put the assignment in his briefcase. When I saw him during the lunch period, he acknowledged that he had reviewed what I wrote and he made clever references to what I wrote.

I was scheduled for his class at the end of the school day. He kept coming to my desk and whispering all sorts of references to my paper. Now keep in mind, I was 12 and I didn't really know all that I wrote on those front and back pages. Some I read from a book and others I learned from experience with He #2. The school day came to an end and that's when I received "The Invitation". He, who we will now identify as He #3, invited me into a vault that was shared by other teachers and was the place where they stored supplies and would use the manually operated ditto machine. This was dangerous, yet I was so trusting. The thing about predators is that they tend to gain the trust of their prey before they pounce. So here I was, in this dark vault, at 12 years old, with a grown man who began to kiss me and then asked, "Do you want me to put it in?" For some reason, at that point I became very fearful and I managed to say "No." The next day, I received another invitation to the vault, we re-entered, he kissed me again, and asked me again "Do you want me to put it in?" This time I said "Ok, we'll try". I went through a whirlwind of emotions: I was confused, happy, nervous, and conflicted. He created a bed with a bunch of sports uniforms that had been cleaned. The encounter began and when it was over, I was happy to have made it through.

Later on, I pondered on what took place and I wondered what in the world had I done and what had I gotten myself into? These encounters with He #3 would take place quite frequently and I had convinced myself that this grown man loved me. He had lulled me to sleep in his fantasy world. I was addicted to him, his scent, his sound and his humor, but I was 12 years old and he had two children who were essentially my age. This was insane, and yet exhilarating. I thought I was special because he was adored by adults and students, but he "chose" me. I was book-wise, but life ignorant. I had experienced so much by that point in my life, yet there was so much more left to learn. I did confide in a few people regarding this experience and the word traveled. The more I became aware of others knowing, the more I became ashamed. The encounters ceased once I had moved on from that school in 1992, when I was 13 years old. It was tough to transition, but it was surely one of the best things that could've happened in my life.

Chapter Six
Behind Closed Doors

Throughout my life's journey, I've found myself in some very unique situations. I recall my first summer job experience at the tender age of 14. As an aspiring physician, I took advantage of the opportunity to attend a high school that offered a high school curriculum. It was a school within a school. The school had established a partnership with the Washington Urban League. This partnership created opportunities for those whose career goals were health care related. Based on our career goal, a hospital was chosen for us to be able to spend our time as summer youth employees. My career goal initially was to become a pediatrician and there was a hospital very close to my residence. The only thing is that the hospital was fairly small and didn't include a pediatric ward. The closest thing that was available was a Family Health Center located within the hospital. I was happy with that option: primarily because I could walk to work from home in a matter of minutes.

There was a group of us who were assigned to this particular hospital for our summer jobs. I was the only one, however, to be assigned to the Family Health Center. I was also the baby out of the group. Since, I was skipped in the second semester of the 3rd grade, I started high school at an early age and graduated at 16. At the time I started working at my first summer job, it was at the end of the 10th grade school year and was just a few months shy of turning 15 years old. Because I was just 14 years old, I was only eligible to work for 4 hours. I loved the atmosphere so much that I would volunteer for 4 hours and work a full 8-hour day. Having a servant's heart started pretty early in life for me and I loved being a part of an organization where the primary goal was to encourage wellness and improve health.

There were a few different specialists who worked in the Center. Soon a pediatrician had joined the team. We seemed to not really connect as well as I had connected with the other providers, which was odd, since she was operating in the field, I wanted to be a part of. I'm not sure, but now that I think about it, this actually could've been one of the things that inspired me to change my mind about my career goal. She wasn't as approachable or welcoming as some of the other physicians. Many of the doctors were outgoing and were well liked by their colleagues, the non-clinical staff, and the patients. One of the doctors was of Middle Eastern descent. I believe he was Iranian. He was extremely kind and smiled often. He also was very soft spoken. There was another physician who was very animated. He was Filipino, had a sonorous voice, and liked to joke around a lot. For some, his personality may have been just a tad overwhelming, but he ensured that the work day was not boring. There were a few other physicians who worked at the center too who were pretty outgoing.

The nurses at the Center were also pretty amicable. There were two who I had grown very close to. I had grown so close to one of them that I spent a Thanksgiving with her and her family one year and I would also spend the night at her house some weekends. She had two daughters and three sons. Her youngest child was one of her two daughters. I was deeply saddened to hear the news of her death as she had battled with cancer for a long time. Though, I'm grateful I have fond memories of our times together. She was like another mother to me. She actually was responsible for me tasting venison on that Thanksgiving Day I spent with her. I had made my plate and after having eaten, she said: "So, how did you like that deer meat?". I assured her that I didn't have any deer meat. She insisted that I did. I found out that what I thought was roast beef was actually deer. She found that extremely funny and could barely stop laughing at my naiveté. I must say, she was an excellent cook…so much so that she was able to trick me into eating venison without saying one word. Oh, the memories!

Now, back to those physicians. There was a brother and a sister who both practiced medicine at the Center. I can't be too certain, but I believe they were Jamaican. The sister did not speak very often, but she was pleasant. The brother spoke quite a bit and was known to crack a dirty joke or two. All of the ladies seemed to have an affinity for him because he had what I suppose would now be referred to as swag. He loved the ladies as much as they loved him. He had no problem "being fresh" as some would say back then. He was a little more than fresh, though. In typical predator style, he lured me into his office for what turned out to be a lunch break quickie. Let that sink in: a doctor and a minor (a 14-year old girl) having a "quickie" in an office shared by other doctors who could've walked in and witnessed this crime in action. The truth is no one else ever came not that time or any other time. No one else in the center had any idea of what happened behind closed doors. Behind the closed door was little ol' Danielle and He#4. If you are reading this and may be thinking: "Why didn't you tell someone?" or "Why didn't you yell for help?". I would venture to say that you are not alone in your thinking, but if you have not walked in the shoes of a survivor, it's hard to understand the steps of a survivor. There is a lot that goes on behind many closed doors that has a way of being kept on the hush. What must be understood in most of the instances in my life is that the adults were well liked people and, in my mind, I stood the risk of being somehow blamed or not believed. Much goes on in the mind of a survivor and, in a twisted way, it's usually the protection of the offender. Speaking for myself, this was often the train of thought. But, in spite of these multiple offenses that could've resulted in some people being behind bars, I just kept on moving through life with a façade of everything being ok.

Chapter Seven
The Curse

I remember going through quite a few phases during my teenage years when it came to fashion. At one point, I was into black garments with zippers. I even had black clogs with zippers. I also went through a black and white polka dot shirt phase. Then there was the all black phase. It was so bad that my father actually told me to not buy another black article of clothing. It seemed like black had been the popular choice. Perhaps it was that I was subconsciously in mourning as I functioned and looked fine on the outside yet was dying on the inside. I found that I began to be drawn to wearing extremely baggy clothes. At one point, I was wearing oversized sweaters that belonged to my father and jeans baggy enough to fit two more pair of pants under it. Could it be that I was trying to hide under layers on the outside? Could it have been an artificial means of me protecting myself?

No one ever held a gun to my head, yet I felt helpless when approached by He #1, He #2, He #3, and He #4. There were other "He's" before I reached the age of 16, which is the age of consent. There was the one who hid on the other side of the brick wall when I took a shortcut home from the corner store. He jumped from the other side of the wall and fought to remove my clothes. I fought him back and fortunately, all he was able to do was pull my shirt over my head and then he fled the scene. There was another "He" who would insist on giving me a ride home when I would visit a family member who he was in a relationship with. Before leaving out of the door, I would give the family member a look because I wanted her to accompany him in taking me home, but "He" would insist on leaving out alone with me. "He" had a van and parked it in some area and decided to invite himself to what did not belong to him. What was up with all of these He's who felt as if I was an easy target? How did I become marked as such easy prey? Surely, this must've been a curse. There were no physical weapons and no threats, yet I was struck with the fear that I must comply and meet the demands of these He's. There certainly was a pattern and if you observe patterns long enough, you'll discover the deeper meaning. Could these experiences all be a part of a generational curse?

These were the things that went through my mind. I'd also ask the infamous question: "Why me?" To be a person with a compassionate heart, to be a person who genuinely loved people, to be a person who worked hard to excel academically; why was I having these experiences that damaged some relationships and that were consuming me on the inside? I was a mess: a public success, but a private failure. The girl who graduated high school and started college at the age of 16 seemed to be doing just fine, but she was holding on to these dirty little secrets and telling herself and others that little white lie: that she was ok. The truth was, she was fading…fast. She kept a smile, but it was just a mask to hide the hurt, disappointment, unworthiness, sadness, guilt, and shame she was feeling on the inside. Who was her advocate? Who was looking out for her? Who was on her side? Who wrapped her in their arms and wasn't trying to woo her into an exchange for their fulfillment? Who discerned behind the smile and good grades that there was brokenness beneath the surface? Who came to the rescue of the little girl trapped inside of the body of one who was coerced to grow up fast? These were questions that I never uttered, but often pondered.

I never wanted to be a burden, I never wanted to cause any hurt or harm to anyone, I never wanted to be viewed as anything other than one who helped and one who was caring: yet the perception became the total opposite of what I wanted it to be. I felt not only like a victim, but like a victim who was being re-victimized. It wasn't by harsh words, but it was by dirty looks and silence: though there was a short time frame when words were less than kind. The one man, who I should have been able to depend on, was disappointed when he became aware of some of these occurrences and his verbal response was crushing. He said: "You make it really hard for me to like you". Those words made me sad and angry at the same time and they stung more than the effects of any of the offenses. Yet, I managed to continue to live the lie of making everyone think I was ok.

As a mother of three teens, it causes me to reflect on my years when I was their age and my desire is that their teenage years don't mimic the internal battles I was fighting. In our home, we encourage conversation and are very transparent when it comes to sharing life experiences. It's, in a sense, an effort to break the curse of silent suffering.

Chapter Eight
The Blessing

One thing I've learned in life is that the closer you get to God, the more you see things from His perspective. I've lived long enough and through enough to understand that bad things happen to good people. I'm reminded of the biblical account of Tamar, who was raped by her half-brother, yet there was a lack of response from the man she should have been able to trust most to protect her and look out for her. The thing about Tamar's story, though, is that she silently suffered until death. There was no evidence of restoration or of new life. I'm grateful that my story didn't end that way. After all that I encountered both from the offenses and from the experiences attached to them, I did discover the Light. I learned to acknowledge Him and to develop a dependency on Him. When I lived life my way, in my own strength, I was losing my life. I thank God that I have finally found my place in Him. While I suffered emotional damage, there was no damage that was beyond the repair of His capable hands. In Him, I have found the love, contentment, joy, and safety that I was in need of and I found the identity that I was in search of.

Still compassionate about others and desiring for them to be well and to help them to learn, I have availed myself to be used by God. I've allowed my mess to be turned in to a message of hope, my test to be converted into a testimony, and my frustration to become a vehicle of inspiration to others. Through Christ, I triumphed over my trials and I identify as a victor and not a victim. I am a V.O.I.C.E. (Victorious Overcomer Inspiring Christian Empowerment) and I've been afforded the privilege to launch a ministry with that very title: a ministry that seeks to serve women of any age who have been sexually assaulted or abused. It is to help others to know that they do not have to suffer in silence as I once did. It's to let them know that they have a voice and it matters. The goal is not to focus on the offense, but to understand that "1) you are not alone, 2) it wasn't your fault, and 3) you will overcome." I do my best to encourage, enlighten, and empower others in any way to both discover and walk in their divine purpose. From the Danielle's Place blog created as a platform to share my life experiences to encourage others, to the D.E.W.™ Refreshment Call where a message to encourage application of God's Word in daily living is shared each weekday morning; I choose to allow the Light of God to shine through me. I did not let being violated make me bitter or stress me to death, but I allowed it to somehow make me better and lead me to life.

Most teenagers don't really know who they are purposed to be or what they are destined to do, but I had an idea; it just happened to be clouded with so many other consuming thoughts. Though innocence and a peaceful childhood were taken from me, I've found that God has restored the years!

The brokenness that I once felt inside has been eradicated and I have now been made whole. Daily I am renewed with a holy boldness and a perfect peace. Thanks to God's chemical laboratory of redemption, all of the guilt, shame, and doubt have been wiped out. I no longer suffer in silence, but I use my voice as an instrument of praise and healing. I no longer desire to hide in the Punchout, but I safely dwell in the presence of God. I recognize how I have made some choices in my life that were displeasing to God, yet He loved me. As I consider His lovingkindness and mercy towards me, I've found no other choice than to drop the "F" bomb on those who I may have once had ill feelings towards. I used to be concerned with disappointing my earthly father, who has now transitioned; but I understood the greater importance of living a life that is pleasing and acceptable to my Heavenly Father. Just as He has caused me to have an authentic smile, I want Him to smile because I've chosen to live a life poured out and let all the things I've experienced work together for my good and the greater good. I'm sharing my story so that there is no mistake who it is that deserves the glory. As my great friend says, what we experience in life is either God arranged, or God allowed. I do not know God's full reason for allowing me to experience all that I did, but like Job who was greatly afflicted; my latter is more blessed than my beginning. That's not a secret or a lie!

APPENDIX A
Scriptures for Healing

- *"He heals the brokenhearted and binds up their wounds [curing their pains and their sorrows]."*
Psalm 147:3 (AMPC)

- *"Pleasant words are as a honeycomb, sweet to the mind and healing to the body."*
Proverbs 16:24 (AMPC)

- *"A happy heart is good medicine and a cheerful mind works healing, but a broken spirit dries up the bones."*
Proverbs 17:22 (AMPC)

- *"Then shall your light break forth like the morning, and your healing (your restoration and the power of a new life) shall spring forth speedily; your righteousness (your rightness, your justice, and your right relationship with God) shall go before you [conducting you to peace and prosperity], and the glory of the Lord shall be your rear guard."*
Isaiah 58:8 (AMPC)

- *"And He said to her, Daughter, your faith (your [a]trust and confidence in Me, springing from faith in God) has restored you to health. Go in [b](into) peace and be*

continually healed and freed from your [[c]distressing bodily] disease."
Mark 5:34 (AMPC)

APPENDIX B
Songs for Healing and Restoration

A Heart That Forgives by Kevin LeVar

Healing Streams by Judith Christie McAllister

Healing by Richard Smallwood & Vision

I'm At Peace by Vickie Yohe

Make Me New by Preashea Hilliard

Perfect Peace performed by Marvin Sapp

Place of Healing by Freddy Rodriguez

APPENDIX C
Poems for Healing

Made in His Image

Crafted by the Master's hands
I am fearfully and wonderfully made
My beauty is deeper than the surface
Yet my skin is the perfect shade

He has made me in His image
I am unquestionably divine
From head to toe, I'm glad to know
That I am His glorious design

I am who God says I am
I'm not what the enemy tries to make me to be
I am whole, I am healed,
And with His spirit I am filled
I am the image of the greater He in me.

Free

Your box I don't fit in
My dreams are too tall
Your thoughts try to constrain me
Your mindset...too small

The gifts I've been granted cause me to be free
To serve a limitless God and be all I was created to be

I was not created to be in bondage, so I refuse to be bound
I was created to be free to worship and it's in Christ that my freedom was found

Don't try to put me in that box because I just will not fit
It took too long to get out of the box and I don't miss being in it one bit

I'll sing because I'm happy
I'll worship because I'm free
I'll set my affections on things above and continue to be content with being me

S.P.E.A.K. V.I.C.T.O.R.Y

S.P.E.A.K. V.I.C.T.O.R.Y.
Set goals
Pursue your purpose
Eliminate negativity from your life
Align with God's word
Keep going, in spite of obstacles

View trials as catalysts
Ignite your faith
Commune with God consistently
Thank God in every situation
Overcome hurts
Reject your flesh
Yearn for the things of God

Glory After This

To everything in life there's a purpose and a season

All that you experienced happened for a reason

You are not alone, available to you is support

Don't believe the enemy, because the truth he distorts

You've defied many odds and God has gotten the glory

Bad things may have happened, but that's not the end of your story

You survived all the past dark days, but your life is not done

Morning has appeared and this battle you have won

The weapons may form, but you're in the Master's hands

He'll preserve your life and your pain He understands

Clean Heart

Consecrate me
Anoint me
Cleanse me
Wash me
Make me holy
Purify me

Wash me thoroughly from my iniquity and cleanse me from my sin
Purge me with hyssop, purify me within
Create in me a clean heart and renew a right spirit in me
Cast me not away from Thy presence and take not Thy Holy Spirit from me

Consecrate me
Anoint me
Cleanse me
Wash me
Make me holy
Purify me

On This Day

On this day, I decree & declare that...

My PAST hurts and failures will not have rule over my emotions and actions
My PRESENT discomforts and frustration will not push me away from God's will, but will propel me further into it
My FUTURE success will not make me forget the One who brought me to it, but will cause me to sing His praises all the more

Who Is God?

Who is God? God is love
He sends His angels from above
To guide and protect us in all of our ways
To keep us from stumbling throughout our days
He's everything that we need Him to be
He's Lord of all eternity
He's Alpha & Omega...the beginning & the end
He's a way maker, healer and a faithful friend
He's provider, protector and deliverer too
He's watchful and is mindful of all that we do
He's our rock, our fortress...He's merciful and kind
He's righteous and gracious and gives us peace of mind
He's holy, incomparable...Father to us all
He's there to catch us at the times when we fall
He's compassionate and hears our hearts when they cry
He's a comforter and He wipes every one of our tears dry
Again, who is God? He's just and He's true
His love is unconditional, and He's concerned about you

Choices

Make excuses or make a difference
Get right or get left
Be strong or be Stuck
Be bullied or be bold
Subtract or be distracted
Be focused or be fooled
Be wise or be outwitted
Stand for righteousness or fall for anything

The choice is yours…

His Word

His Word EMPOWERS...
Philippians 4:13 (AMP)
I have strength for all things in Christ (the living Word) Who empowers me. I am ready for anything and equal to anything through Him Who infuses inner strength into me; I am self-sufficient in Christ's sufficiency.

His Word ENCOURAGES...
Joshua 1:9 (AMP)
Have not I commanded you? Be strong, vigorous, and very courageous. Be not afraid, neither be dismayed, for the Lord your God is with you wherever you go.

His Word ENLIGHTENS...
Psalm 119:105 (AMP)
Your word is a lamp to my feet and a light to my path.

His Word ENDURES...
Mark 13:31 (AMP)
Heaven and earth will perish and pass away, but My words will not perish or pass away.

Things to Do

MOTIVES...check them
WORDS...wisely choose them
FRIENDS...survey them
GOOD FRIENDS...keep them
THOUGHTS...examine them
PRIORITIES...properly order them
PROMISES...honor them
PROBLEMS...yield them
PEOPLE...love them
DREAMS...believe in them
OBSTACLES...overcome them

Moving Forward

Respect is earned
Discipline is learned
Lessons are taught
Opportunities are to be caught
Work is to be done
Battles are to be won
Words of faith ought to be spoken
Bad habits ought to be broken

Let's not just await divine intervention
Let's begin to move forward with diligent intention

No More Shackles

Unchained from my past
no longer have I shame
Been labeled by many
but I've claimed a new name
The guilt has been banished
the burden has been lifted
No longer a slave
to where my mind & soul once drifted
Delivered from strongholds
that once had me bound
Was lost in sin
but because of Christ am now found
No longer afraid
of how by others I am viewed
My heart has been changed
my spirit renewed
I've got a new walk
in light and liberty
No longer captive, nor afraid...
my new name is FREE!!!

Possibilities

Curses, chains,
and bad habits can be broken
When venom is spewed,
words of life can be spoken
Ponder not on what isn't,
but on what can be made so
There's still room for a "yes",
even if 100 times you've been told no
Obstacles can be overcome
and battles can be won
Speak the Word, pray in faith,
and watch His handiwork be done
Miracles didn't end
with thousands being fed by a considerably small meal
Many more have since been performed
and they are unquestionably real
I'm convinced all things are possible
and every day miracles are done
How do I know? I've seen Him do it...
Trust and believe: I am indeed one!

Necessary

In the mornings when I'm lying down in my bed
and the sun rises and shines upon my face
I see the magnificent radiance of God's beauty
and the evidence of His amazing grace
Yet another day to be alive
and to be a vessel used for His glory
Adding more pages to the book of my life
entitled "God's Transformation by Grace Story"
He loves, He sees, He cares about me
and knows all of the challenges I've faced
But by His perfect Love, sent from above,
those challenges I've both endured and embraced
There's no one like Him, He's a sovereign God
and with Him there is no failing
In spite of my labor pains, what shall be birthed,
will be worth all of the travailing

It was necessary...

Metamorphosis

I started low and slow
Crawling to find my way
To my next meal
I would get full
But not of what was nourishing
I consumed the lies that were being fed to me
Like a poisonous leaf
The lies were toxic
But I was built for adversity
I was attacked, but not destroyed
I got connected to the True Vine
I began to grow
I shed my old skin
A wall of protection was created around me
I began to change
Into a new creation
I developed wings
I no longer crawl
I rise above the ugly past
I fly high
In the beauty of the now

Still Standing

Misused for selfish desires
They tried to break me
The branch was only a small part of the tree
I'm firmly planted
My roots run deep
The soil is rich
The river of Living Water is my supply
Some branches may have been broken
Some branches may have been shed
But I'm still standing

The Wilderness

In the wilderness we feel deserted.
Our souls thirst.
We feel alone.
We feel abandoned.
We get restless.
We are vulnerable.
We suffer.
We complain.
We miss being connected.
We miss everyday luxuries.
What we really miss is the lesson, though.
In every wilderness, there is provision.
While feeling disconnected from the world,
The Ultimate Connector reveals Himself.
Our eyes open.
We see Him.
We come to know Him more intimately.
The experience isn't just to try us,
It's to transition us.
Turns out,
The wilderness was just what we needed.
It prepared us for what was to come.

Note to Self

Remember to say "Thank you"
Remember to be kind
Not just to others
But keep YOU in mind
Quitting is not an option
At least not for you
Remember to celebrate the small victories
To help you get through
Pat yourself on the back
Give yourself a high five
You did it! You didn't quit!
You survived! Now thrive!
Destiny awaits
Though the journey may be long
Pace yourself, but do not quit
Make sure you finish strong!

Calm

The day was crazy
Things have been moving too fast
I haven't had time to catch my breath
My thoughts won't slow down
The cars around me won't speed up
I love music
But right now it sounds like noise
Can someone please turn the volume down
The cars start to move faster
The thoughts haven't slowed down
I'm closer to my destination, though
I keep going until I get there
I park
I take in the scenery
I get out and the music begins to play
It's the sound of the birds singing
It's the sound of the water brushing against the rocks
It's the sound of the nearby bell ringing on the hour
It's the sound of nature
Suddenly the thoughts become still
Then it finally hits me
I'm calm

Yesterday

Yesterday I was afraid
Yesterday I said I couldn't
Yesterday I was worried
Yesterday I said I wouldn't
Yesterday has come and gone
Today is a new day
I realize that I was oh so wrong
To ever part my lips to say
That I couldn't or that I wouldn't
Those are words of defeat
Today I can and today I will
No matter how bittersweet

Lotus Lessons

Fragrant
Beautiful
Precious
Unfavorable surroundings
Yet, she stands tall
She rises above the muddy waters
Her leaves are pristine
Though the mud surrounds her
She is unbothered
She grows and people around her admire her beauty
They admire her strength

Growing Pains

I'm comfortable where I am.
I do not want to leave.
However, there is a very sad truth:
I have no room to breathe.
The pot has unfortunately become too small.
My growth is becoming stunted.
I find I just don't fit at all,
It's like I'm no longer wanted.
I try to wrap my brain around it.
I guess I just need room to grow.
It's so hard to say goodbye,
but in order to live I must go.

If A Diamond Could Talk

A diamond is one of the most treasured jewels.
Its brilliance shows forth a radiant glory
that causes eyes to widen and smiles to form.
As it sits atop a band, it speaks volumes...
it's viewed as the symbol
of one person's heart being touched so much
that they want to spend forever with another.
A diamond is said to be a girl's best friend.
It is indeed highly valued,
but what we see and treasure so much is the finished product...
we are not privy to the process
and would maybe reject what a diamond looks like in the beginning.

A rough diamond,
or a diamond that has yet to be properly prepared and tested,
is dull and does not exhibit the beauty that it has the potential to possess.
There is a preparation process.
However, that is required
to cause a diamond to have that sought after brilliance.
The very formation of a diamond is a process within itself.

A diamond is formed under the circumstances of extreme heat and immense pressure.
Its brilliance is the result of both cutting to shape it and then polishing.
Essentially, what we see is the glory,
but we don't know its story.

If a diamond could talk, it would probably say something like this:
"*You don't know my story.*
You don't know the things that I've come through.
You cannot imagine.
The pain the trials I've had to endure."

The fact that we do get to see the glorious jewels in stores and on the hands of friends, family, and passersby
is because someone did see the beauty and the value in the rough diamond.
Someone saw what shall be and embraced the rough diamond
and allowed it to carefully go through the process of becoming.

We are like those diamonds.
To most, they may see the glory of God's anointing shining through us,
but they have no idea of the shaping and polishing required for the anointing.

Furthermore, they have no idea of the rejection you went through
when you didn't look like what you shall be.
BUT GOD!!!
God who created us, knew what we shall be...
before we were formed in the womb
just as He did Jeremiah.
"Before I even formed you in your mother's womb, I knew all about you. Before you drew your first breath, I had already chosen you to be My prophet to speak My word to the nations." - Jeremiah 1:5

An actual diamond can't talk.
You, Jewel, can.
Don't be afraid to share your testimony
and let others know how God chose you
when you were in the rough
 and how He shaped and polished you
so that you can show forth His glory.
When you do so,
you help others know that they too can be shaped and polished...
no matter how rough they may be.
Where others may reject us,
He thinks we are worth it.

Breaking the Silence

As Min. Michelle D. Bennett shared in the beginning, it's been my prayer that you absorb what's shared and feel safe to reveal your truth. This book confidently assures that you are not alone in this life's journey. Below you will find a space to share and break the silence of any dirty little secret or little white lie you have been holding on to. Remember, in sharing:

There's no shame. There's no bondage. There is only freedom.

_____
_____
_____
_____
_____
_____
_____
_____
_____
_____
_____
_____
_____

About the Author
Danielle N. Hall

Danielle N. Hall is an advocate for all to recognize and achieve their divine purpose. She is continually looking for ways to enlighten, encourage, and empower others through this journey called life. She is a sexual abuse survivor and the visionary/founder of V.O.I.C.E. (Victorious Overcomers Inspiring Christian Empowerment). She is the sole author of her debut book "Dew Drops: Refreshing for the Soul". Additionally, she has been a contributing author of 3 projects: She Wouldn't Let Me Fall (2018), Hope for the Overcomers Soul (2018) and My Whole Self Matters Empowerment Journey Journal (2019). She is a married mother of 3, who endeavors to both achieve and maintain balance given the demands of family, work, ministry, and self.

Facebook: Author, Danielle N. Hall
IG: @daniellenhall1
Twitter: @DanielleNHall1
LinkedIn: Danielle N. Hall
Email: mrsdaniellehall@yahoo.com
Online: www.daniellenhall.com

About the Publisher
Vision to Fruition Publishing House

At Vision to Fruition, we are dedicated to helping others bring their personal, business, ministry & nonprofit visions to fruition.

Whether it's as grand as a book you want to write, a business you want to start, a conference or event you want to host, a ministry you want to launch or an organization you want to start; or as small as needing a computer repair, logo design or web design; Vision to Fruition will help you walk through the process and set you up for success! At Vision to Fruition we don't have clients, we have Visionaries. We provide solutions to equip others to pursue their visions & dreams with reckless abandon.

In we have successfully published more than twenty-three authors, eight of which were Amazon Bestsellers. We would love for you to join our family of Visionaries as well!!!

Phone: 240-343-3563
Facebook: Vision to Fruition
Email: info@vision-fruition.com
Online: www.vision-fruition.com

www.ingramcontent.com/pod-product-compliance
Lightning Source LLC
LaVergne TN
LVHW041633070426
835507LV00008B/601